KEEP
CALM
AND
USE AN
AFFIRMATION

**Compiled by
Cameron McCool**

Fifty per cent of the proceeds earned from the sale
of this book will go directly to the Hay Foundation.

HAY HOUSE
Australia • Canada • Hong Kong • India
South Africa • United Kingdom • United States

First published and distributed in the United Kingdom by:
Hay House UK Ltd, 126–134 Baker Street, First Floor, London W1U 6UE.
Tel.: (44) 20 8962 1230; Fax: (44) 20 8962 1239.
www.hayhouse.co.uk

Published and distributed in the United States of America by:
Hay House, Inc., PO Box 5100, Carlsbad, CA 92018-5100.
Tel.: (1) 760 431 7695 or (800) 654 5126; Fax: (1) 760 431 6948 or (800) 650 5115.
www.hayhouse.com

Published and distributed in Australia by:
Hay House Australia Ltd, 18/36 Ralph St, Alexandria NSW 2015.
Tel.: (61) 2 9669 4299; Fax: (61) 2 9669 4144.
www.hayhouse.com.au

Published and distributed in the Republic of South Africa by:
Hay House SA (Pty), Ltd, PO Box 990, Witkoppen 2068.
Tel./Fax: (27) 11 467 8904. www.hayhouse.co.za

Published and distributed in India by:
Hay House Publishers India, Muskaan Complex, Plot No.3, B-2,
Vasant Kunj, New Delhi – 110 070. Tel.: (91) 11 4176 1620; Fax: (91) 11 4176 1630.
www.hayhouse.co.in

Distributed in Canada by:
Raincoast, 9050 Shaughnessy St, Vancouver, BC V6P 6E5.
Tel.: (1) 604 323 7100; Fax: (1) 604 323 2600

Text © Louise L. Hay, Gabrielle Bernstein, Stephanie Butland, Ali Campbell, Marie-Claire Carlyle, Laura Leigh Clarke, Joseph Clough, Arielle Essex, Kyle Gray, Judy Hall, David R. Hamilton, Robert Holden, Davina Mackail, Blue Marsden, Simon Middleton, Jacky Newcomb, Seka Nikolic, John C. Parkin, Louise Presley-Turner, Martin Shirran, Shed Simove, Jenny Smedley, Gordon Smith, Steve Taylor, David Wells, John Whiteman, 2012

The moral rights of the authors have been asserted.

A catalogue record for this book is available from the British Library.

ISBN: 978-1-78180-105-5

Printed and bound in Great Britain by TJ International Ltd, Padstow, Cornwall

MIX
Paper from
responsible sources
FSC® C013056

CONTENTS

INTRODUCTION

Within this book is a collection of original, soothing affirmations, designed to help you heal and create positive outcomes in many areas of your life.

Affirmations are powerful. The moment you say them, you are no longer helpless. You are acknowledging your own power. An affirmation is the starting point to your healing, to your success. It opens the way. You are saying to your subconscious mind: 'I am taking responsibility. I am aware there is something I can do to change.'

If you continue to use the affirmation, either you will be ready to let whatever it is go and the affirmation will come true, or it will open a new avenue to you.

I am delighted to share my affirmations alongside many other original affirmations from leading Hay House UK authors. I encourage you to recite these affirmations daily at a time that suits you. Using positive affirmations with consistency will help you cultivate a strong base of unconditional love and self-acceptance from which to live your life. Over time, you will naturally begin to replace negative thinking with kind words and positive, supportive thoughts.

You can also consult *Keep Calm and Use an Affirmation* when you need guidance in the present moment; simply ask for help and open the book to find an affirmation to support you. Whether you're new to affirmations, or you are fully aware of their transformative power, I know you will benefit from this book. So that others may also benefit, 50 per cent of the proceeds earned from the sale of this book will go directly to the Hay Foundation.

I love you, and all is truly well,

Louise L. Hay

Love
Your
Work

I work for enjoyment
and satisfaction, not just
to earn a living.

LOUISE L. HAY

The doors of opportunity
are always open in my career.
I am thrilled to serve!

KYLE GRAY

I am aligned with
my life purpose and
rewarded financially for
the value I deliver.

LAURA LEIGH CLARKE

$\mathcal{M}$y job is perfect for my schedule. It is easy and fun for me to be productive and organized at work.

LOUISE L. HAY

I choose to do work that sustains and nourishes me, and I appreciate the worth of the work that I do.

STEPHANIE BUTLAND

My work space is a sacred haven. I treat it with respect and love.

LOUISE L. HAY

I am skilled at finding happiness and joy in everything I do. I am the source of happiness, joy and peace in my life.

DAVID R. HAMILTON

I understand that I have the right to be successful and happy.

SHED SIMOVE

$\mathcal{M}$y success is my
gift to the world.

ROBERT HOLDEN

$\mathcal{T}$oday I choose to see
solutions instead
of problems.

JOHN WHITEMAN

I give myself permission to have the greatest day of my life. It's great to be my own boss!

GORDON SMITH

$\mathscr{P}$eople respect me and
are very appreciative of
everything I do.

LOUISE L. HAY

I allow my talents to come forwards, and I work with them to make my fortune.

LAURA LEIGH CLARKE

My work is an expression of love.

I can be of great service to others and make money at the same time.

LAURA LEIGH CLARKE

Harmonize
Your Home

My home is my sanctuary protecting my family and me at all times. I allow only the highest vibrations of love to reside in my home.

LOUISE PRESLEY-TURNER

I thank my present home for sheltering me so comfortably. My heart is at home here.

LOUISE L. HAY

I surround myself only with objects and colours that make my body vibrate with joy. I am in perfect balance with my home and myself.

JACKY NEWCOMB

The Angels surround my home in a pure, harmonious light. My home is filled with love.

KYLE GRAY

Housework is fun.
I always have the time
to spruce up my home.
I love doing simple chores.

LOUISE L. HAY

$\mathcal{I}$clear the old to

embrace the new.

MARIE-CLAIRE CARLYLE

My home is a reflection of my inner state. So sometimes I must clean the mirror.

JOHN C. PARKIN

I bless my home.
I put love in every corner.

LOUISE L. HAY

I am an oasis of peace, harmony, prosperity and laughter. My home reflects all that I am.

DAVID R. HAMILTON

My home fulfils all my needs and desires. I infuse my living space with the vibration of love.

LOUISE L. HAY

My home is a place of harmony where my thoughts resonate with vibrations of joy, peace and love.

ARIELLE ESSEX

My home is a peaceful haven. All is well in my home and in my world.

LOUISE L. HAY

I love my home and my
home loves me!

MARIE-CLAIRE CARLYLE

Experience
More Love

*L*ove is the lifeblood of the Universe – it can never run out. There is always more love so I give it freely with a wide-open heart.

DAVINA MACKAIL

I am blessed with infinite love and gratitude.

LOUISE L. HAY

I feel love all around
me. I am love, I love
and I am loved.

LOUISE PRESLEY-TURNER

As I radiate love towards others, I bring more love into my life. As I love more, I am loved more.

DAVID R. HAMILTON

$\mathscr{I}$am truly someone
special. I love myself.

LOUISE L. HAY

$\mathcal{T}$he Angels of Love
surround my life as I open
my heart to receive!

KYLE GRAY

$\mathcal{I}$ am immersed in love.

STEPHANIE BUTLAND

When I complain less
and appreciate more,
I find it easy to love more
and fear less.

ARIELLE ESSEX

My path is not to find a
lover but to be love.

GABRIELLE BERNSTEIN

I love unconditionally,
starting right here and
now with me.

ALI CAMPBELL

$\mathcal{M}$y love is limitless.

LOUISE L. HAY

I allow love to shine into all corners of my relationships today.

LOUISE PRESLEY-TURNER

I bless everything I come across today with acceptance and love.

LOUISE L. HAY

Happiness is a choice. Love is a choice. I'm choosing them both.

SIMON MIDDLETON

I naturally gravitate towards people and activities that make my soul sing.

Flow Gracefully with Change

New and joyous
experiences are a part of life,
and through them all, I am
safe. It is only change.

LOUISE L. HAY

I welcome change with open arms, knowing that the universe has my back. I manifest a blessed and abundant life with each new change I make.

LOUISE PRESLEY-TURNER

Everything I do is
by choice.

LOUISE L. HAY

In any situation I ask
myself 'What would I
LOVE to have happen?'
Life doesn't get better by
chance; it gets better by my
choosing to change.

DAVINA MACKAIL

When I relax and listen
to my body's signals,
they effortlessly guide me
to where I need to go.
I am excited by the new
opportunities that await me.

JACKY NEWCOMB

*E*verything I need comes
to me in the right time
and space sequence.

LOUISE L. HAY

I let go of my need for certainty and control. I expand my possibilities and allow space for the magic and mystery of life to find me.

DAVINA MACKAIL

$\mathcal{I}$ am willing to
change and grow.

LOUISE L. HAY

$\mathcal{I}$ ask angels for help, and even if I'm temporarily confused by the direction of life, I always accept that change is leading me to my rightful destination.

JENNY SMEDLEY

$\mathscr{I}$ am flexible. I welcome change in my life and adapt with courage and ease.

DAVID R. HAMILTON

I recognize and embrace change as the natural state of the world.

STEPHANIE BUTLAND

*I*t is easy for me to get centred. Even in the midst of stress, I can relax.

I am exactly where I need to be. There is a plan; I just don't know what it is yet. I trust the process.

JUDY HALL

When one door closes,
another one opens.
I always have access to
the One Infinite Source,
and I am safe.

LOUISE L. HAY

*I*t's time to give up swimming and let the river carry me.

STEVE TAYLOR

Boost
Self-Esteem

I love and accept myself
in every way, exactly as I am.

I am willing to see only my magnificence.

I have everything I need right here within me. I am perfect exactly as I am.

JUDY HALL

I am the most important person in my world, and the only one I need to impress.

JENNY SMEDLEY

When I take care of myself, everyone around me benefits. I lavish myself with love and acceptance. I am an amazing, unique and wonderful human being.

LOUISE PRESLEY-TURNER

I can be anything and do
anything I choose –
and I choose to be
the best me possible.

MARTIN SHIRRAN

I stop struggling to be better. I accept myself as someone who is supported by everyone and everything around me. All is well.

LOUISE L. HAY

I give myself absolute permission to be absolutely happy, right now.

ALI CAMPBELL

$\mathcal{I}$ believe in myself and know that my self will return the favour.

DAVID WELLS

I am powerful beyond
my dreams.

JOHN WHITEMAN

I say 'F**k It' to self-doubt and go for what I love in life.

JOHN C. PARKIN

When I catch myself searching for happiness, looking for love or chasing success, I gently remind myself 'I am what I seek.'

ROBERT HOLDEN

When I accept myself just as I am, I find the courage to be who I came here to be.

ARIELLE ESSEX

$\mathscr{I}$ am welcome wherever
I go, and I am totally
adequate at all times.

LOUISE L. HAY

I allow myself to shine knowing I deserve only the best!

KYLE GRAY

I'm worth it. Not because
I use a certain shampoo.
But because I am.

JOHN C. PARKIN

I love being me.

LOUISE L. HAY

Manifest
Financial
Prosperity

This is a delightful day.
Money comes to me
in expected and
unexpected ways.

LOUISE L. HAY

*T*oday I have endless opportunities to receive.

GABRIELLE BERNSTEIN

I am emotionally at peace with my financial situation. I am open to divine guidance, which perfectly leads me to new opportunities, insights and ideas that bring increased wealth into my life.

LOUISE PRESLEY-TURNER

I find it easier and
easier to make, receive
and enjoy money.

LAURA LEIGH CLARKE

I am worthy of a very good income. There is no need to struggle to achieve it; it comes easily to me.

LOUISE L. HAY

Infinite love and
infinite abundance are
my birthright.

BLUE MARSDEN

I welcome abundance
into my life with open arms;
I release all blocks and know
that I deserve good now.

LOUISE PRESLEY-TURNER

I have a good
relationship with money,
and I always have enough
for my needs.

LOUISE L. HAY

I focus on giving rather than receiving – I give selflessly and I receive more wealth in every area of my life.

JOSEPH CLOUGH

My true abundance isn't based on my net worth; it's based on my self-worth.

I support other people in becoming prosperous, and in turn life supports me in wondrous ways.

LOUISE L. HAY

$\mathscr{I}$ am worthy of riches.
Money is energy, as am I.
I fully accept myself and
money flows to me.

JOSEPH CLOUGH

$\mathscr{I}$ allow any and all resistance to receiving money to come up and evaporate.

LAURA LEIGH CLARKE

I give myself permission
to be prosperous.

*T*oday I practise
vocal gratitude, saying
'thank you' out loud for
life's many blessings.

ROBERT HOLDEN

Heal Your Body

$\mathcal{I}$am at home in my body.
It is safe for me to relax and
to be at peace right here,
right now.

LOUISE L. HAY

$\mathscr{I}$'m grateful to my body for all the amazing things it does every single second, to keep me healthy and alive.

STEVE TAYLOR

My body is an oasis of health. Vitality continually and effortlessly flows through my blood vessels, bones, tissues and cells, delivering health and longevity to all that I am.

DAVID R. HAMILTON

I go within and connect with that part of myself that knows how to heal.

LOUISE L. HAY

I am well.
I will be well.
I will stay well.

STEPHANIE BUTLAND

$\mathcal{M}$y mind can heal my body. It's the thought that counts.

DAVID R. HAMILTON

$\mathcal{I}$ can heal this; I have the power. I feel that belief in every cell of my body. I believe it!

JUDY HALL

My spine glows bright, my internal organs sigh, each tiny cell is smiling and relaxed. Unconditional love returns me to my divine blueprint of health.

All that I need to help
me on my healing pathway
is here now.

LOUISE L. HAY

Healing energy radiates
through every cell, chakra
and meridian in my body.
It's good to be alive today!

LOUISE PRESLEY-TURNER

$\mathcal{I}$can feel my heart
smiling.

ROBERT HOLDEN

Every cell in my body responds to every thought I think. My immune system knows I love myself, so it identifies with vibrant health.

LOUISE L. HAY

I have a healthy body by maintaining a healthy mind. I have a healthy mind by maintaining a healthy body.

SEKA NIKOLIC

Thank you Angels for the healing that has already been given to my being!

KYLE GRAY

My body understands what it needs, and I listen to it and answer those needs.

STEPHANIE BUTLAND

Forgive Yourself and Others

$\mathscr{I}$ release all the junk
from the past. I live in
the present moment.

LOUISE L. HAY

I let go of my regrets, and understand that mistakes made by me and by others are all learning opportunities.

JENNY SMEDLEY

The past is over, so it has no power now. The thoughts of this moment create my future.

LOUISE L. HAY

Forgiving someone who hurt me doesn't mean I am letting him or her off the hook – it means I am letting go of the pain they caused.

STEVE TAYLOR

$\mathcal{W}$hen I forgive someone
it sets me free.

ROBERT HOLDEN

I release all old hurts
and forgive myself.

LOUISE L. HAY

I forgive anyone who has wronged me at any time and I accept forgiveness from those I have wronged. I profoundly love, accept and forgive myself.

JUDY HALL

I allow others to
be themselves.

LOUISE L. HAY

*O*ur hearts know only
love and forgiveness.
From my heart I forgive you.
May you find peace.

$\mathcal{W}$hen I make a mistake,
I realize that it is only part
of the learning process.

$\mathcal{I}$ am grateful for the experiences of my past. I release all past hurts and embrace the present with happiness and joy.

DAVID R. HAMILTON

$\mathscr{I}$am compassionate
and understanding.
I forgive and forget.

LOUISE L. HAY

I always look to find the best in myself and others. This makes it easy to forgive and be forgiven.

SEKA NIKOLIC

$\mathcal{M}$y heart is open.
I speak with loving words.

LOUISE L. HAY

I surrender my past
knowing the spirit of
forgiveness fills my core.
It is safe for me to let go.

KYLE GRAY

Connect to
Spirit

$\mathscr{I}$create miracles in
my wonderful world.
I am open to the wonders
of the universe.

LOUISE L. HAY

I am made of the same material as the stars. The spirit of the universe connects with me easily and naturally when I accept this.

JENNY SMEDLEY

I remember now that underneath it all I am spirit, and have just been playing the game of forgetting who I really am.

JOHN C. PARKIN

As I look around me,
I see the universe in all
things, and I breathe in the
awareness that I am
the universe.

DAVID R. HAMILTON

I see evidence of God's grace wherever I am.

ROBERT HOLDEN

My guides are always
with me. I am safe.

LOUISE L. HAY

Each thought I have creates an energy flow within and around my physical being.

GABRIELLE BERNSTEIN

Magic happens all the time. I expect it, believe it and have faith in it. I live in a truly miraculous and magical universe.

DAVINA MACKAIL

I breathe deeply and fully. I take in the breath of Life, and I am nourished.

LOUISE L. HAY

I bathe in the divine light at the heart of the universe – the universal whole, the sea of Spirit to which we all belong.

JUDY HALL

$\mathcal{I}$am connected with
a higher power.

LOUISE L. HAY

I breathe in the living energy that exists all around me. All the power that ever was or will be is here now.

DAVINA MACKAIL

*D*aily ritual reconnects
my soul to my spirit and
to God.

DAVID WELLS

I am not the thoughts inside my head, I am the stillness in between.

JOHN WHITEMAN

I am fully connected to the divine. I am a spark of divinity manifesting beingness… I am one with the onlyness. I am that… I am…

BLUE MARSDEN

CONTRIBUTING AUTHORS

Louise L. Hay is the author of the international bestseller *You Can Heal Your Life*. She is a metaphysical lecturer and teacher with more than 50 million books sold worldwide. For more than 30 years, she has helped people throughout the world discover and implement the full potential of their own creative powers for personal growth and self-healing. She has appeared on *The Oprah Winfrey Show* and many other TV and radio programmes both in the USA and abroad. **www.louisehay.com** and **www.healyourlife.com**

• • • • • • • • • •

Gabrielle Bernstein is the No. 1 bestselling author of the books *Add More ~ing to Your Life*, *Spirit Junkie* and *May Cause Miracles*. Described as 'a new role model', Gabrielle is also the founder of the social networking site herfuture.com, which inspires, empowers and connects women worldwide. **www.gabbyb.tv**

Stephanie Butland writes and blogs about how thinking differently helped in her dance with cancer. She is the author of *How I Said Bah! to cancer* and *Thrive: the Bah! Guide to Wellness After cancer*.
www.bahtocancer.com

....

Ali Campbell is the internationally bestselling author of *Just Get On With It* and *More than Just Sex*. A licensed master and trainer of neuro-linguistic programming, life coach and hypnotherapist, he is a trusted advisor to international celebrities, rock stars and even royalty.
www.alicampbell.com

....

Marie-Claire Carlyle is the author of *How to Become a Money Magnet* and *Money Magnet Mindset*. Marie-Claire is passionate about empowering you to live a life that is worthy of you. She is an inspired speaker and believes that we can find a solution to global poverty in our lifetime.
www.marieclairecarlyle.com

Laura Leigh Clarke is a business and money coach to the heroes of the entrepreneurial revolution, and that means YOU! Author of *Wire Yourself for Wealth*, she coaches heart-centred solopreneurs who are ready to make more money doing what they love to do.
www.wireyourselfforwealth.com

Joseph Clough is a certified master practitioner of neuro-linguistic programming and hypnosis. Author of *Be Your Potential*, he is passionate about helping others transform their lives and achieve their dreams. Joseph is also the producer of 100+ hours of free audio dedicated to your transformation, found on his site.
www.josephclough.com

Arielle Essex has worked as a healer for over 25 years, practising various forms and specializing in mind–body psychology. She is the author of *Compassionate Coaching*, and her story features in *The Living Matrix* documentary.
www.practicalmiracles.com

Kyle Gray is The Angel Whisperer. Blessed by the presence of angels since the age of four, Kyle became the UK's youngest professional psychic medium at the age of 16. Today he works tirelessly to give approachable and understandable advice and insight to heaven, always delivered in his natural, up-front style. His first book, *The Angel Whisperer,* is out now.
www.kylegray.co.uk

• • • • • • • • •

Judy Hall has been a karmic astrologer, past life explorer and crystal wonder-worker for 40 years. Author of the books *Psychic Self Protection, The Crystal Bibles (1, 2 and 3), 101 Power Crystals, Good Vibrations* and *Crystal Prosperity,* Judy recently appeared on the *Watkins Review* list of the 100 most spiritually influential people of the century.
www.judyhall.co.uk

• • • • • • • • •

David R. Hamilton PhD spent four years developing drugs in the pharmaceutical industry. Now the author of seven books, including *How Your Mind Can Heal Your Body* and *Is Your Life Mapped Out?,* he gives lectures and workshops around the world that help people to understand the role of their mind and emotions in all areas of their lives.
www.drdavidhamilton.com

Robert Holden's innovative work on psychology and spirituality has been featured on *The Oprah Winfrey Show* and in two major BBC TV documentaries – *The Happiness Formula* and *How to Be Happy*. He is the author of *Happiness NOW!*, *Shift Happens!*, *Be Happy*, *Authentic Success* and *Loveability*.
www.robertholden.org

. . . .

Davina Mackail BA Hons, RGN, DFSNI is Channel 5's dream expert with regular appearances on *The Wright Stuff*, *The Vanessa Show* and *Live with Gabby Logan*, and is the author of *The Dream Whisperer* book and CD. Besides running a busy practice for private and business clients, she teaches advanced feng shui and is the former Dream Columnist for the *Daily Mail*.
www.askdavina.com

. . . .

Blue Marsden is the author of *Soul Plan: Reconnect With Your True Life Purpose*. He is also a psychotherapist, hypnotherapist and chi kung teacher who runs the Holistic Healing College and the London School of Chi Kung. Blue's unique spiritual/holistic counselling training combines conventional counselling with Soul Plan reading and the latest healing modalities into one professional qualification.
www.healingcollege.co.uk

Simon Middleton is one of the UK's leading experts on brands and branding. Author of the book *Brand New You*, Simon's consultancy firm Brand Strategy Guru advises companies and charities all over the world.
www.simonmiddleton.com

· · · · · · · · ·

Jacky Newcomb is a multi-award-winning, bestselling author and motivational speaker. She is the angel and afterlife columnist for *Fate & Fortune* magazine, frequently features in the national press and is a regular guest expert on radio and TV. Jacky has produced hundreds of articles on paranormal phenomena, and has taught thousands of people – including grief counsellors, nurses and doctors – about angels and the afterlife.
www.jackynewcomb.com

· · · · · · · · ·

Seka Nikolic is the author of two Hay House titles, *You Know More Than You Think* and *You Can Heal Yourself*. She is recognized as the UK's No. 1 Bio-Energy Practitioner and is celebrated all over the world for her exceptional powers. Widely referred by doctors and specialists, she treats patients suffering from a huge range of ailments from sports injuries to various medical conditions, and her success rate is phenomenal.
www.sekanikolic.com

John C. Parkin is the author of the bestselling *F**k It* books, which have been translated into 22 languages. Ten years ago he and his wife, Gaia, said F**k It to top jobs in London and escaped to Italy. They now bring the F**k It message to a global audience in the form of F**k It Retreats (in Italy), F**k It Music, online courses and even F**k It Chocolate.
www.thefuckitlife.com

· · · · · · · · · ·

Louise Presley-Turner is one of the UK's leading life coaches, and author of the book *Finding a Future That Fits*. Louise has helped to turn around the lives of numerous clients who, perhaps like you, were tired of feeling trapped by their current circumstances. Her unique style of coaching is known for producing amazing results.
www.thegameoflife.co.uk

· · · · · · · · · ·

Martin Shirran is the co-author of *Pause Button Therapy* and *The Gastric Mind Band*. Martin most enjoys writing when sitting on the balcony of his home in southern Spain, watching the sun set over the inspiring mountain ranges of Andalucia.
www.pausebuttontherapy.com

Shed Simove is an author, serial entrepreneur and corporate speaker on creativity and innovation. Shed has sold over one million products worldwide, and his books include *Success… or Your Money Back*, *Presents Money Can't Buy* and *Ideas Man*.
www.shedsimove.com

. . . .

Jenny Smedley is the author of 20 books, eight of which were inspired by angels. She lives in the beautiful Somerset countryside with her husband, her pet sheep, chickens and ducks, and her dog, KC.
www.jennysmedley.com

. . . .

Gordon Smith is an astoundingly accurate medium, renowned for his ability to give exact names of people, places and even streets relevant to a person's life. Author of *Intuitive Studies: A Complete Course in Mediumship* and several other bestselling titles, Gordon travels around the world demonstrating his abilities and offering healing and comfort to thousands of people.
www.gordonsmithmedium.com

Steve Taylor is the author of several bestselling books on psychology and spirituality, including *The Fall, Waking From Sleep, Out of the Darkness* and *Back to Sanity*. Eckhart Tolle describes Steve's work as 'an important contribution to the shift in consciousness that is happening on our planet at present'. Steve is also a poet, and his first book of poems – *The Meaning* – was published in 2012.
www.stevenmtaylor.co.uk

· · · · · · · · · ·

David Wells is an outstanding astrologer, past life therapist and Qabalist, and the author of several books on psychic and spiritual development, including *Your Astrological Moon Sign* and *21 Days to Understanding the Qabalah*.
www.davidwells.co.uk

· · · · · · · · · ·

John Whiteman is an inspirational speaker who teaches ancient wisdom in a modern world, both personally and in business. Author of *9 Days to Feel Fantastic*, John is the creator of The Way and The Enlightened Business. His aim is simple: to make a difference to as many lives as possible.
www.johnwhiteman.com

JOIN THE HAY HOUSE FAMILY

As the leading self-help, mind, body and spirit publisher in the UK, we'd like to welcome you to our family so that you can enjoy all the benefits our website has to offer.

 EXTRACTS from a selection of your favourite author titles

 COMPETITIONS, PRIZES & SPECIAL OFFERS Win extracts, money off, downloads and so much more

 LISTEN to a range of radio interviews and our latest audio publications

 CELEBRATE YOUR BIRTHDAY An inspiring gift will be sent your way

 LATEST NEWS Keep up with the latest news from and about our authors

 ATTEND OUR AUTHOR EVENTS Be the first to hear about our author events

 iPHONE APPS Download your favourite app for your iPhone

 HAY HOUSE INFORMATION Ask us anything, all enquiries answered

join us online at **www.hayhouse.co.uk**

 126–134 Baker Street, First Floor, London W1U 6UE
T: 020 8962 1230 E: info@hayhouse.co.uk